Inner Trauma Transformation

A 365 day Journal of Affirmations for the Mind, Body & Soul

Rewire Your Subconscious Mind for

Healing, Positivity & Success

Kimberly Walters

Introduction

I wrote this book because I was born into adverse circumstances. Both of my parents were negatively impacted by the crack epidemic. Due to inability to cope with their trauma, my parents developed mental illness and resulted in long term substance abuse. As a result, my parents were unable to care for me so I was placed in foster care, at the age of five. After moving from house to house, I was eventually adopted at the age of 9 years old. I suffered emotional, physical, and sexual abuse while in foster and adoptive care; causing me to struggle with suicidal ideation and behavior. Feeling isolated and deeply depressed and thinking that I was a total waste of life, by the age of 10 I actively planned on committing suicide. The day I chose to act on my plans of suicide, my mother switched up my after school routine and took me to the library to borrow a new book. I asked the librarian for help this time around, as I had read the entire collection of Huckleberry Finn books; which were my favorite at the time. The librarian handed me a book called "The child called IT" by David Peltzer. Little did I know, the story in the book not only would change my plans but save my life and change the trajectory of my entire life.

As years passed by, I tried my best to avoid my painful past by achieving success, in every aspect of my life. It wasn't until I was diagnosed with clinical depression, anxiety, and PTSD, due to childhood trauma, that I would be forced to deal with the pain of my past. So I began talk therapy; which supported me to cope with what I was experiencing. After several months of counseling sessions, I began to feel better, to a degree. I still experienced harsh critical self-talk, self-doubt, and suicidal thoughts; which impacted how I cared for myself and my family. It was then that I realized that I needed to do more for myself. Although therapy helped to unveil deeply rooted trauma, It was then that I discovered the healing power of affirmations; which led me to becoming the woman you see today.

I wrote this book to support you in transitioning from trauma survivor to trauma thriver so that you can become a better version of yourself and live purposefully from the inside out. This book includes all of the affirmations I have spoken to rewire my subconscious mind in the process of me transitioning from a trauma survivor into a trauma thriver.

You can thrive emotionally and mentally and recover fully from the negative effects of trauma. You can live a life full of love, joy, peace, and prosperity. It starts today. These 365 affirmations are powerful and work to support you to heal your mind,body, and soul from the pain of the past by rewiring your subconscious mind for healing and positivity.

If you need more support than this book can provide alone, book a call with me to see how we can support you in becoming the best version of yourself and living purposefully from the inside out.

Www.KimberlyWalters.co

Kimberly Walters, Life Coach, Author, Entrepreneur

Note to the reader..

"Positive affirmations open the door for change and can transform your thinking, your belief systems, and your way of life.

Essentially what you are saying to your subconscious mind is, "I am taking responsibility for my own actions and I am aware that there is something I can do to change my life."

When I talk about affirmations, I mean consciously choosing words that will either empower you to eliminate something from your life or support you to create something new in your life.

What I've learned is, every time you think a thought and every word you speak is an affirmation, believe it or not. All of our negative self-talk and negative chatter, is a stream of affirmations that we are using in every moment of our life, which disempowers us, creating negative experiences in our lives.

It is important to remember that not only are you affirming but you are creating your life experiences with every word and thought. Your beliefs are simply habitual thinking patterns that you learned as a child.

Many of them work very well for you and many of them do not, limiting your ability to create the things you say you want. What you want and what you believe you deserve may be two totally different things.

It is important to pay attention to your thoughts so that you can begin to eliminate the ones creating experiences you do not want in your life.

By reading these affirmations, daily you are taking the first step towards living purposefully from the inside out. I know you can do it, I believe in you!"

-Kimberly Walters

Here is a small practice for yo...

The times of day to achieve the best results with reprogramming your subconscious mind is in the morning, as soon as you awake and right before you sleep

When you are in a drowsy state, pockets of your subconscious mind are open and readily available for reprogramming

This is when your subconscious mind is in Theta state, readily available to rewrite its beliefs

I designed these affirmations in a way where you can start gaining confidence in yourself and progressing to experiencing the greatness that you have from within; living purposefully from the inside out

I recommend that you read these affirmations for a minimum of 21 days, observe how you react after stating the affirmation

Notice the extra writing space beneath each affirmation. Journal how the affirmation made you feel, what thoughts came up for you?

Last but not least dear, be gentle with yourself and trust with consistency your life will improve for the better.

Day 1. I am present today and every day to change unhealthy habits into healthy habits.

Day 2. I fill my cup with love and care everyday before I tend to others.

Day 3. I am blessed with this life. I am available to more good than I have experienced in life.

Day 4. I am connected to my whole self and I am in harmony with my entire being.

Day 5. I am unique and I am an incredible person.

Day 6. I am free to express my truth and I am centered in my truth.

Day 7. I am powerful. I create my own reality with each new thought I think.

Day 8. I am an excellent friend to myself.

Day 9. I am an exceptional human being doing the best that I can do in the present moment.

Day 10. I am embracing all of who I am.

Day 11. I am saying kind things to myself with a smile on my face and love in my heart.

Day 12. I am joy, I am light, I am free. I am openhearted and I lead with my heart.

Day 13. I am at peace and I am in love with who I am.

Day 14. I am living a meaningful life and I am trusting life.

Day 15. I am so happy and grateful now that I am learning from inner wisdom and allow it to guide me to make good decisions.

Day 16. I am so happy and grateful now that I am evolving and improving everyday.

Day 17. I am obedient. I listen to my inner voice and I choose to make wise choices day by day.

Day 18. I am light. I am radiating the light that I shine.

Day 19. I am so happy and grateful now that my light shines bright and I allow myself to be a light for others.

Day 20. I am so happy and grateful now that I am car reality with my thoughts and actions.

Day 21. I am mindful and I live in the present moment.

Day 22. I am intentional and I'm living my purpose on earth. I am strong enough to be all that I can be.

Day 23. I am worthy and deserving of the very best. I am accepting that I can create my reality.

Day 24. I am confident in myself and my skills and I am loving my uniqueness and my talents.

Day 25. I am full of potential and I am gifted.

Day 26. I am growing gracefully and thriving mentally, physically, emotionally, and financially.

Day 27. I am worthy of all of my dreams and I am capable of achieving all of my goals.

Day 28. I am so happy and grateful that I am courageous, magnificent, and brilliant.

Day 29. I am aligned in my beliefs, words, acts, and core values. I am integrity.

Day 30. I am counting my many blessings each and every day.

Day 31. I am aware of all that I am and all that is possible for me.

Day 32. I am open to life's care of me. I am loved.

Day 33. I am expressing my wants and communicating my needs.

Day 34. I am in flow with the rhythm of life.

Day 35. I am ready to accept the best and nothing but the best.

Day 36. I am loving my life and I am moving in harmony with the rhythm of life.

Day 37. I am steadily achieving greatness. I am giving and receiving love.

Day 38. I am an inspiration to others and I am proud of who I am for myself and for others.

Day 39. I am motivated and committed to become the very best version of myself.

Day 40. I am remarkably wonderful and brilliant.

Day 41. I am a highly blessed soul that is eager to reach my fullest potential.

Day 42. I am centered in my truth as I release limited beliefs and nourish thoughts of growth.

Day 43. I am making good decisions consistently.

Day 44. I am an observer of my thoughts and my feelings.

Day 45. I am educated, intelligent and I am wise. I am brilliantly created to succeed in life.

Day 46. I am dedicated, well-organized and persistent. I rule my day, each and everyday.

Day 47. I am making the most out of every hour of my day.

Day 48. I am defying all odds and statistics stacked against me.

Day 49. I am demanding the best from myself each and every day.

Day 50. I am understanding and patient in my evolution.

Day 51. I am healthy and balanced in mind, body, and soul.

Day 52. I am strong. I am nourishing my body as the vessel of my spirit.

Day 53. I am feeding my mind the best education possible.

Day 54. I am healthy, inside and out and I am revitalized in energy.

Day 55. I am soothing myself when I quiet my mind.

Day 56. I release thoughts of the past and of the future.

Day 57. I am beautiful and brilliant and I am acting on my creativity.

Day 58. I am endlessly enthusiastic about life.

Day 59. I am expressing the happiness of life and I am connected to my inner knowing.

Day 60. I am connected with my guidance.I am manifesting all of my dreams, goals, and desires.

Day 61. I am commanding my life and I am taking my power back and changing for the best.

Day 62. I am sure with my intentions. I set purposeful intentions each and every day.

Day 63. I am decisive in all acts and I am making the most of all opportunities.

.

Day 64. I am accountable for all of my creations.

Day 65. I am connected to all people for they are connected to me.

Day 66. I am aligned with my beliefs, words, and acts. I am in love with life.

Day 67. I am in flow as I create a rewarding life for myself and my loved ones.

Day 68. I am in flow and building momentum with every goal I accomplish.

Day 69. I am light and I am full of positive energy.

Day 70. I am materializing my beliefs, effortlessly and easily.

Day 71. I am persistent and resilient. I am determined to make the most out of my life.

Day 72. I am patient. I am bold. I am brave, I overcome challenges again and again and again.

Day 73. I am a portion of the world's wisdom and I am walking towards my dreams.

Day 74. I strive to make my dreams a reality each and every day.

Day 75. I am manifesting a better day everyday. I am well on my way to becoming my best self.

Day 76. I am evolving to my truest self.

Day 77. I am evolving into the better version of myself as I am limitless in my thinking.

Day 78. I am worthy of occupying space.

Day 79. I am limitless when it comes to creating good health and wealth into my life.

Day 80. I am a good person. I am very secure with myself.

Day 81. I am confident in my ability to make positive changes in every aspect of my life.

Day 82. I have very high self esteem. My self esteem is growing day by day.

Day 83. I value and honor my boundaries by saying "yes" to myself.

Day 84. I believe in myself and I believe in my abilities to take action each and every day.

Day 85. I am in control of my life. I am creating a beautiful life for myself, full of joy and peace.

Day 86. I am full of possibilities and I am infinite possibilities.

Day 87. I am intentional and I set and achieve my goals daily.

Day 88. I deserve to be happy, successful, and wealthy.

Day 89. I am worthy of love and attention

Day 90. I am confident, believing in myself comes naturally to me. I am unique and I have unique abilities.

Day 91. I am valuable, every day my self worth is growing.

Day 92. I am worthy of having healthy relationships with people who want the best for me.

Day 93. I am positive; therefore I attract good things in my life.

Day 94: I love people, people are attracted to being with me because they see the good in me.

Day 95. I am respectful of my boundaries and people respect me because I have boundaries.

Day 96. I am worthy of respect and appreciation and I deserve to be treated with respect.

Day 97. I am attractive and people respect me for who I am as an individual.

Day 98. I am love and I respect myself for who I am. I am worthy of love, success and happiness.

Day 99. I am a trailblazer and I make a difference in the world. I have wonderful talents to share with the world.

Day 100. I am worthy of making my dreams come true.

Day 101. I am amazing and I have greatness and potential within me.

Day 102. I am valuable and I value my worth. I deserve having what I want in life.

Day 103. I am powerful and I have the power to change my circumstances in every aspect of my life.

Day 104. I am love and I love the person I am becoming. I am consistent with improving every day in every way.

Day 105. I am decisive and I make good and wise decisions about my well being.

Day 106. I am successful and I believe in myself and my abilities to create wealth for myself.

Day 107. I am radiant and self confident; being confident comes easily to me.

Day 108. I am safe when I'm near other people and I can be tranquil in every situation.

Day 109. I am peace and I practice being at peace with myself and others.

Day 110. I am positive, by changing my thoughts I create peace in my world.

Day 111. I am forgiving of myself. I release judgement of myself and others.

Day 112. I am present. I choose to let go of the past and open my heart to love again.

Day 113. I am where I'm supposed to be. I believe everything happens for a reason and for my greater good.

Day 114. I am excited to start a new page in my life.

Day 115. I am attracted to loving people. I attract people who accept me and love me for who I am.

Day 116. I am limitless. I allow my heart to guide me because it is limitless.

Day 117. I am whole and healthy. I create time and space to heal my mind, body, and soul.

Day 118. I am full of love and I'm learning to love myself unconditionally, more and more every day.

Day 119. I am focused on the positive aspects of my life.

Day 120. I am happy now that I know life wants the best for me and I allow happiness to enter my world.

Day 121. I am grateful for all of my emotions as they teach me valuable lessons.

Day 122. I am powerful and mighty beyond measures. I release my past and reclaim my power.

Day 123. I am free and I'm giving myself the gift of freedom from the past and moving with joy into the future.

Day 124. I am always learning as I am a lifetime learner.

Day 125. I am compassionate, as I embrace love and empathy for myself and others.

Day 126. I am courageous and I courageously embrace the good in my life and in myself.

Day 127. I am the master of my inner and outer world.

Day 128. I am enthusiastic and I move into the future with joy and enthusiasm.

Day 129. I am strong and my heart, mind, and body are getting stronger each day.

Day 130. I am healthy and my health and wealth is improving each and every day.

Day 131. I am in great shape, spiritually, physically, and emotionally.

Day 132. I am whole and my body is capable of healing itself.

Day 133. I am so happy and grateful now that I am healed. I allow myself time and space for my body to heal.

Day 134. I am gentle and kind with myself through my self discovery journey.

Day 135. I am capable of manifesting a life I love. I believe in my ability to manifest happiness and healing in every aspect of my life.

Day 136. I choose to create healthy habits and make healthy choices in my life today and everyday.

Day 137. I am so happy and grateful now that everything in my life is working in my favor.

Day 138. I am intuitive and self aware. I view every emotion as guidance to my healing.

Day 139. I am of essence. I am beautiful. I am love.

Day 140. I am mighty and powerful and I have the power to process what happened to me.

Day 141. I am wise. I'm learning valuable lessons from mistakes, making me wiser and stronger.

Day 145. I am a seer and I am a visionary.

Day 146. I am intuned with my guidance and I learn from every situation to heal, evolve and grow.

Day 147. I am intentional and I intend to set boundaries with others to protect my wellbeing.

Day 148. I am so happy and grateful now that I am stronger.

Day 149. I am independent and self-sufficient.

Day 150. I am free and I accept the things I can change and release the things I cannot change.

Day 151. I am positive and I'm changing in positive ways.

Day 152. I am compassionate and kind. I am a being of love and light and I allow for myself to love myself and others.

Day 153. I am loved and lovable. I am light and I allow for my light to shine no matter what.

Day 154. I forgive myself for not spending time with myself.

Day 155. I am powerful and I have the power over my own life. I have the power to heal my wounds, my wounds are healing.

Day 156. I am trusting of myself and of others. I am becoming stronger each and every day.

Day 157. I am important and I matter to myself and others. I am excited about this new beginning.

Day 158. I am capable of loving again and I am learning to love myself unconditionally.

Day 159. I am enough. I have a lot to offer and I can find happiness in any situation.

Day 160. I am so happy and grateful now that I know everything is unfolding as it is supposed to. I am grateful for the lessons of life.

Day 161. I am honorable and lovable. I am deserving of love from myself and from others.

Day 162. I am excited to start my new life as I choose happiness, health, wealth, and harmony.

Day 163. I am joy and I enjoy spending time with myself. I am free to become the best version of myself.

Day 164. I am likable, lovable, and worthy of love.

Day 165. I am grateful and I allow myself to feel joy, to experience laughter, and to smile out of gratitude.

Day 166. I am a seer, I show up today and everyday to create healthy habits and set boundaries to support my growth.

Day 167. I am kindhearted, I allow my heart to open up to new possibilities. I am capable of trusting others because I trust myself.

Day 168. I am attractive, positive and healthy relationships are coming into my life.

Day 169. I am worthy of loving people, beautiful places and things.

Day 170. I am valuable, I add value to every room I walk in. I embody confidence and high self esteem.

Day 171. I am worth putting myself first and giving myself the time, love, and space to heal.

Day 172. I am peace, finding peace in myself as I connect with my intuition is important to me.

Day 173. I am whole, I heal my wounds more and more every day, as I surrender to the healing process.

Day 174. I am capable of positive change, I allow myself to let go and trust the process of change.

Day 175. I am beautiful, inside and out. I am valued and have high self esteem.

Day 176. I am of high self esteem, I hold my head up high while I heal my emotional wounds.

Day 177. I am aware of my needs, I nurture the relationship that I have with myself first.

Day 178. I am love, I am willing to open my heart to share the love that I have to offer.

Day 179. I am loved and I am loveable. I am limitless and so is my heart.

Day 180. I am honest with myself and everyone around me.

Day 181. I am integrity, resilient, and I am full of strength.

Day 182. I trust myself and listen to my intuition.

Day 183. I am trustworthy, I trust and believe in my talents and skills to make things better wherever I go.

Day 184. I am excellent. I am strong, courageous and worthy of all great things.

Day 185. I am stronger, wiser and more confident with each new day.

Day 186. I am knowledgeable, I do the best that I can do with the knowledge that I have.

Day 187. I am the CEO of my life, I fire and hire people into my life as I choose.

Day 188. I am capable of setting healthy boundaries, I stand up for myself by saying how I truly feel with kindness and love.

Day 189. I am a gift to others, I'm becoming the person I know myself to be.

Day 190. I am confident, I radiate with confidence in all that I do.

Day 191. I am brave, I ask for what I want in life.

Day 192. I am courageous and I take action and follow through.

Day 193. I am capable of creating positive experiences for myself. I forgive myself for holding onto painful memories.

Day 194. I forgive myself and release my past and the things I cannot change.

Day 195. I am free. I am healthy. I am wealthy. I can manifest my dreams and achieve my goals.

Day 196. I forgive myself and others. I am capable of greatness and creating a life full of new positive experiences.

Day 197. I am so happy and thankful now that my faith is unwavering.

Day 198. I am grateful for all of the good that surrounds me.

Day 199. I am so happy and grateful now that I intend to live each day to the fullest.

Day 200. I am so happy and grateful now that I embrace good thoughts. I am a positive thinker. I am optimistic.

Day 201. I am grateful for my life, the people in it and all that is possible for me.

Day 202. I am full of infinite possibilities. I am capable of moving forward in life and manifesting my dreams.

Day 203. I am ready to make positive changes and I am open to new and exciting opportunities.

Day 204. I am a creative being, I'm cocreating my destiny. I receive positive change and new opportunities.

Day 205. I am so happy and grateful now that I'm becoming a new and improved version of myself.

Day 206. I am supportive, I'm supporting my success and I am supported by others.

Day 207. I am flow, I'm overflowing with joy, love and gratitude.

Day 208. I am love, I love and accept myself. I celebrate myself and others.

Day 209. I am capable of positive change. I'm shifting, pivoting, and preparing to move forward in life.

Day 210. I am genuine, I open my heart to others by seeing the good in them.

Day 211. I am safe and secure. I believe that there is good in the world.

Day 212. I am worthy of being celebrated. I celebrate myself, others, and all that is right in the world.

Day 213. I am so happy and grateful now that I celebrate myself for all of my achievements and for the love that I share.

Day 214. I am so happy and grateful now that I am growing, evolving and coming into alignment with new things; becoming the person I always knew myself to be.

Day 215. I am worthy of being seen and heard. I allow my light to shine, I radiate with kindness and love in my heart.

Day 216. I am inspirational, I inspire people with my kind words and courageous actions.

Day 217. I am kind, I choose to be kind to myself and everyone I meet.

Day 218. I am open to receiving abundance and prosperity in all its forms. I'm giving and receiving love openly and freely.

Day 219. I am so happy and grateful now that I trust and care for myself. I am in a joyous and loving relationship with myself.

Day 220. I am so happy and grateful now that I live a peaceful life. I am worthy and deserving of love, trust, and peace.

Day 221. I am so happy and grateful now that I am ready for healthy relationships.

Day 225. I am so happy and grateful now that I am loyal to myself and others. I am at peace with myself and others.

Day 226. I release fear and embrace love and joy. I am full of peace, love and happiness.

Day 227. I release unhealthy habits that limit my potential. I am defying all odds as I cocreate my future.

Day 228. I am so happy and grateful now that I am unstoppable on my path to success.

Day 229. I am so happy and grateful now that I can achieve great things because I know that greatness lives in me.

Day 230. I am so happy and grateful now that I live in the present moment. I am releasing painful thoughts of the past.

Day 231. I am responsible for my emotions and how I react to others, I am responsible for how I act and treat others.

Day 232. I am so happy and grateful now that I know that I am endless possibility, I can become who I choose to become.

Day 233. I am capable of positive change. I can transform my life on purpose, easily and effortlessly.

Day 234. I am so happy and grateful now that I know I can redefine who I am again, and again, and again.

Day 235. I am so happy and grateful now that I can own my story and love myself through the healing process.

Day 236. I am so happy and grateful now that I can transform myself, my finances, and my relationships.

Day 237. I am so happy and grateful now that I am evolving. I radically accept change in my life.

Day 238. I am so happy and grateful now that I am choosing to feel good about myself each and every day.

Day 239. I am doing the best that I can with what I have. In every moment I can remind myself that I am doing the best I can.

Day 240. I am so happy and grateful now that I am full of compassion for myself and for others.

Day 241. I am so happy and grateful now that I am focusing on my goals and my vision; steadily working towards the life I desire to have.

Day 242. I am so happy and grateful now that I visualize my best self, today and everyday.

Day 243. I am so happy and grateful now that I am healthy, wealthy, happy, and whole.

Day 244. I am so happy and grateful now that I accept and appreciate the feelings of good health and wellbeing inside of me.

Day 245. I am worthy of attention and praise. I am so happy and grateful now that I am attracting new opportunities in my life.

Day 246. I am so happy and grateful now that I thrive under pressure and flow with what is happening in the moment.

Day 247. I am so happy and grateful now that I always act on my successful ideas, creating abundance and prosperity in my life.

Day 248. I am so happy and grateful now that I am abundant in blessings, peace, and prosperity; which positively impacts my wellbeing for my good and everyone attached to me.

Day 249. I am so happy and grateful now that I am cultivating new healthy habits to support me in creating a life I love.

Day 250. I am so happy and grateful now that I accept and appreciate the abundance in my life.

Day 251. I am so happy and grateful now that I allow myself to feel abundance from the inside out.

Day 252. I am so happy and grateful now that I know I am capable of living a full and abundant life.

Day 253. I am so happy and grateful now that I am full of love for myself and others.

Day 254. I am love and light; love works miracles in my life supporting me to create a life full of abundance and prosperity.

Day 255. I am so happy and grateful now that I am willing to make positive changes in my life.

Day 256. I am capable of positive change, positive changes can begin in this very moment.

Day 257. I am so happy and grateful now that I am pleased with myself and all that I do. I am enough.

Day 258. I am so happy and grateful to know that it is my birthright to live a full and free life.

Day 259. I am so happy and grateful now that I allow my knowledge, skills, and income to constantly expand.

Day 260. I am so happy and grateful now that I am bringing about freedom and stability into my life.

Day 261. I am so happy and grateful now that I am recognizing my body as a dear friend.

Day 262. I am so happy and grateful now that I am taking good care of my body, as it is the vessel of my soul.

Day 263. I am so happy and grateful now that I am creative, and I communicate effectively through expressing myself.

Day 264. I am so happy and grateful now that I am worthy of receiving all good things.

Day 265. I am so happy and grateful that good flows into my life from unexpected and expected sources.

Day 266. I am the creator of my destiny. I am brilliant and remarkable in every way.

Day 267. I am opening my heart and I am willing to let go of all resistance in my life.

Day 268. I am grateful for a safe living space and it is filled with loving thoughts and memories.

Day 269. I am one with the power and wisdom of the source of all mankind. God lives within me.

Day 270. I am so happy and grateful now that I know that I am unlimited in my ability to create a life that I love.

Day 271. I am so happy and grateful that I inhale and exhale freely and fully. I am grateful for my breath. I am grateful for life.

Day 272. I am so happy and grateful now that I know I am capable of achieving my big dreams. I know that I deserve to make my dreams come true.

Day 273. I am having joyful thoughts to help me create joy in my world from the inside out.

Day 274. I am talented and gifted. I allow my abilities to support me to live an abundant life.

Day 275. I am so happy and grateful now that I am handling my emotions in a healthy and positive way.

Day 276. I am so happy and grateful now that I am in control of my emotions and choose to react in a healthy and positive way.

Day 277. I am centered in my truth and I focus on the experiences I desire the most.

Day 278. I am equally blessed with opportunities to improve my life and well being. I am grateful to know that opportunity is everywhere.

Day 279. I am a seer. I visualize the life I desire and take action to create the life I want to live.

Day 280. I am loving my life. I allow my endless supply of love to flow freely.

Day 281. I am so happy and grateful now that I love and cherish my body. I feed my body clean foods and beverages that are nourishing to my body.

Day 282. I am fit. I exercise in fun ways everyday to support me in my wellness journey.

Day 283. I am life. I love life and I am so happy and grateful to be alive.

Day 284. I am so happy and grateful now that I love and honor myself. I am willing to release the need to be and feel validated.

Day 285. I am stepping into my greatness and I am becoming all that I am destined to be.

Day 286. I am so happy and grateful now that I feel good about the people I attract in my life. I am supported by other people and the universe.

Day 287. I am so happy and grateful now that my relationships are loving, healthy, and nourishing to my mind, body, and soul.

Day 288. I am free of burdens, I have great compassion for myself and others.

Day 289. I am so happy and grateful now that I feel safe to go beyond the limitations other people placed on me.

Day 290. I am so happy and grateful now that I am free to authentically be myself. I am thriving in life.

Day 291. I am mindful of my words. I speak words of encouragement and inspiration to myself and others.

Day 292. I am in a space of peacefulness. I am where peace, love, harmony, and good fortune reside.

Day 293. I release the need to feel like a victim. I thrive and rise above all adversity.

Day 294. I am a creative being. I create personal calm for myself, effortless and easily.

Day 295. I am intuitive. I connect with my intuition daily.

Day 296. I release all expectations of myself and others. I expect good things to happen to me and in my life.

Day 297. I am created to be and feel fulfilled. I am so happy and grateful now that I live life with purpose.

Day 298. I am caring for myself the best I know how and I know that I am cared for.

Day 299. I am powerful. I am so happy and grateful now that I know noone or nothing has power over my mind. I am in control.

Day 300. I am exceptional in my strengths. I am learning from my past experiences and are applying the lessons learned in mylife.

Day 301. I am in a sacred relationship with my body. I love that I am a unique being created with love.

Day 302. I am so happy and grateful now that I am the authority of my mind, body, and soul.

Day 303. I am so happy and grateful now that I am rising above all limitations, mentally, emotionally, and physically.

Day 304. I am confident in myself. I believe that I am equipped to live and enjoy a prosperous and abundant life.

Day 305. I am so happy and grateful now that I can smile and feel joy for myself and others.

Day 306. I am so happy and grateful now that I am enjoying my self- discovery journey. I am open to new and wonderful experiences.

Day 307. I am capable of making the right decision. I desire to do the right thing by myself and by others.

Day 308. I am openhearted. I open the gates of my heart, wider than ever before.

Day 309. I am so happy and grateful now that my heart is full of love. I allow large amounts of love to flow from me and to me.

Day 310. I am blessed and highly favored. I am grateful to know that I am safe, secure, and supported.

Day 311. I am safe. I feel great around people and people feel great around me.

Day 312. I am miraculous. I believe in miracles, miracle after miracle is happening in my life.

Day 313. I am open to receiving more miracles in all aspects of my life, today and everyday.

Day 314. I am so happy and grateful now that miracles flow to me and I welcome them into my life with open arms.

Day 315. I release the need to people please. I take care of myself and my needs first.

Day 316. I am looking forward to the future with joy in my heart.

Day 317. I am so happy and grateful now that I have amazing relationships in my life.

Day 318. I am so grateful that the loving friendships I am searching for are searching for me.

Day 319. I am so happy and grateful now that I know that I am a seer and a unique individual.

Day 320. I am so happy and grateful now that I feel safe sitting in silence to connect with myself.

Day 321. I am so happy and grateful now that I connect with my inner knowing each and every day.

Day 322. I am growing and developing myself each and everyday. I intentionally create time to explore myself in a deeper way.

Day 323. I am so grateful that my life continues to show evidence of my growth.

Day 324. I am moving into my greater good. I am living my life's purpose.

Day 325. I am integrity. I act in integrity and honor for myself and others.

Day 326. I am choosing to think positively and believe bigger to create a life I will love.

Day 327. I am full of joy and I am in harmony with all of life.

Day 328. I am so happy and grateful now that I am aware that I am powerful. I choose to use my power wisely.

Day 329. I am so happy and grateful to know that I'm supported by the universe every step of the way.

Day 330. I am worthy of love and I am worth loving. I am surrounded by love.

Day 331. I am radiating good health, wealth, happiness, and peace of mind.

Day 332. I am so happy and grateful now that I am moving beyond limiting beliefs.

Day 333. I am so happy and grateful now that I trust myself to take good care of myself. I am tuned in with my inner voice.

Day 334. I am open to connecting with my intuition. I am trusting my inner guidance.

Day 335. I am well. I believe that there is healing in showing my emotions.

Day 336. I am an expressive human being. I allow for myself to heal and feel my emotions.

Day 337. I am safe and secure in who I am and what I am capable of. I believe that it is safe for me to share my feelings.

Day 338. I am awakening my consciousness to experience the possibilities that life has to offer.

Day 339. I am safe with myself, with others, and in the world.

Day 340. I am adapting to change and growth. I am at ease with knowing that what I need to know is revealed to me at the right time.

Day 341. I am beautiful. I see myself as a bold, and brilliant force who is wise and beautiful.

Day 342. **I am magnificent.** I love what I see when I look into the mirror at me.

Day 343. I am uniquely created. I identify my body as a wondrous work of art, and I feel honored to live in it.

Day 344. I am a priority and I prioritize my needs first and foremost.

Day 345. I am in charge of my life. I am taking my power back and changing for the best.

Day 346. I release judgemental thoughts towards myself and others. I am approving of myself at all times.

Day 347. I am worthy of success. I am deserving of abundance, prosperity, and the very best in life.

Day 348. I am passionate and goal oriented. I deserve to create time for myself to engage in activities that bring me joy.

Day 349. I am worthy and valuable. I am enough. I deserve to achieve all of my goals and live out my wildest dreams.

Day 350. I am accepting of myself and others. I am worthy to be celebrated, recognized, and complimented.

Day 351. I am knowledgeable. I deserve to be acknowledged for my wisdom, it is an honor when people recognize me.

Day 352. I am a gift to others. People love me and treat me with the utmost respect.

Day 353. I am grateful now that I know that intention is what yields a purposeful living.

Day 354. I am processing my emotions to achieve my vision; so that I can become a better version of myself.

Day 355. I am visualizing my best self today and everyday. I am so happy and grateful now that I recognize the value of myself and my life.

Day 356. I am focusing on healing my wounds and becoming the best version of myself.

Day 357. I allow myself to feel all emotions, as they are valid and they deserve my attention.

Day 358. I give myself permission to move forward in life and embrace new experiences with open arms.

.

Day 359. I am stepping out of my comfort zone to explore a new awareness and possibility.

Day 360. I am embracing of freedom and change. I welcome the new with open arms and an open heart.

Day 361. I am comfortable in my body. I am enjoying life in my body and the blessings that I receive with each breath that I take.

Day 362. I am beautiful and so is my body. My body is beautiful and it takes me where I have to go, easily and effortlessly.

Day 363. I am surrounded by loving people who see the good in me.

Day 364. I am so grateful that I am taking action on my goals and creating the life of my dreams.

Day 365. I will react with patience and understanding to my emotions. I am an observer of my emotions and the emotions of others.

Hello! I have a community of amazing women just like you!

Where we strive to thrive in our self discovery journey so that we can become a better version of ourselves, manifest lives we love, and live purposefully from the inside out.

You can join our Heal On Purpose Community, full of purpose driven women

by clicking the link below.

Within this community we will celebrate your wins with you, provide you with additional resources to accompany you in your self discovery journey, and watch you become the best version of yourself; the woman you always knew yourself to be!

We can't wait to see you Lovely!

https://www.facebook.com/groups/731588614395762

About the Author

Kimberly Walters is the CEO & Owner of Walters Consulting & Services, Author, Life Coach and Creator of the personal development brand, Inner Trauma Transformation, She specializes in trauma, mindset, and resilience. She has a unique methodology, stemming from a holistic conscious living approach. Her work is all about empowering women to live purposefully (from the inside out), building resilience to trauma, creating a mindset that empowers, turning their search inwards, creating a loving self-connection, and learning to truly accept and value themselves. Through her books, online courses, workshops, and 1:1 coaching practise she is opening the hearts and minds of women by helping them affirm wellness one day at a time.

Book your Discovery Call today: <u>kimberlywalters.co</u>